*Never
Stop Holding
Hands*

Never Stop Holding Hands

AND OTHER MARRIAGE SURVIVAL TIPS

SHARA GRYLLS

David C Cook®

transforming lives together

NEVER STOP HOLDING HANDS
Published by David C Cook
4050 Lee Vance View
Colorado Springs, CO 80918 U.S.A.

David C Cook Distribution Canada
55 Woodslee Avenue, Paris, Ontario, Canada N3L 3E5

David C Cook U.K., Kingsway Communications
Eastbourne, East Sussex BN23 6NT, England

The graphic circle C logo is a registered trademark of David C Cook.

All Scripture quotations are taken from the Holy Bible, New
International Version®, NIV®. Copyright © 1973, 1978,
1984 by Biblica, Inc.™ Used by permission of Zondervan.
All rights reserved worldwide. www.zondervan.com.

LCCN 2011937598
ISBN 978-0-7814-0670-3
eISBN 978-1-4347-0473-3

First UK edition published as *Marriage Matters* in 2006 by
Pen Press Ltd © Shara Grylls, ISBN 978-1-905203-65-9
Second UK edition published in 2009 © Lion
Hudson, ISBN 978-0-7459-5502-5

The Team: Alex Field, Nick Lee, Renada Arens, and Karen Athen
Cover Design: Amy Konyndyk
Cover Photo: iStockphoto
Illustrations: Charlie Mackesy

Printed in the United States of America
First North American Edition 2012

1 2 3 4 5 6 7 8 9 10

For Bear
You are my everything

Shara was born in 1974, is married to Bear, and is mother to three boys named Jesse, Marmaduke, and Huckleberry. She lives with her family, dividing time between a Dutch barge on the River Thames and a small private Welsh island.

PREFACE

This little book is a compilation of quotes that people gave my husband and me when we got married. We simply asked everyone to enclose with their wedding invitation replies some words that they thought might help us. We were overwhelmed with great advice.

Some of the quotes are made up, and some are classics. There are poems, recipes, sayings, old wives' tales, just simple common-sense advice, and a few special Bible verses I've added, but overall, the outstanding quality that shines through this book is love. In the good times, in the hard times, *love*—being a friend when it really matters, protecting each other.

I love being married and completely adore my husband, and therefore this book is for him … with all my love.

Shara Grylls

ACKNOWLEDGMENTS

Thank you to all our friends and family who contributed these quotes and sayings, and for making this little book what it is. Thank you so much to you, Charlie, for the cartoons; they are, like you, inspired.

A successful marriage requires falling in love many times, always with the same person.

—**Mignon McLaughlin**

"Do you come here
often?"

First—Tell each other you love each other several times each day.

Second—Make each other laugh. Seeing the funny side of things, and of each other, is the best "fuel" for a successful marriage.

Third—Always say to yourself, "How will my actions affect the other?"

May God watch over you always.

—**Bear's Father**

Together,
live each day like your last
and each night like your first.

Never stop holding hands.

Keep a short account of wrongs.

The giving must always
exceed the taking.

From this day forward,
You shall not walk alone.
My heart will be your shelter,
And my arms will be your home.

For this reason a man will leave his father and mother and be united to his wife, and they will become one flesh.

Genesis 2:24

Be best friends.

There is no more lovely, friendly,
and charming relationship,
communion, or company
than a good marriage.

—**Martin Luther**

Send her flowers for no reason.

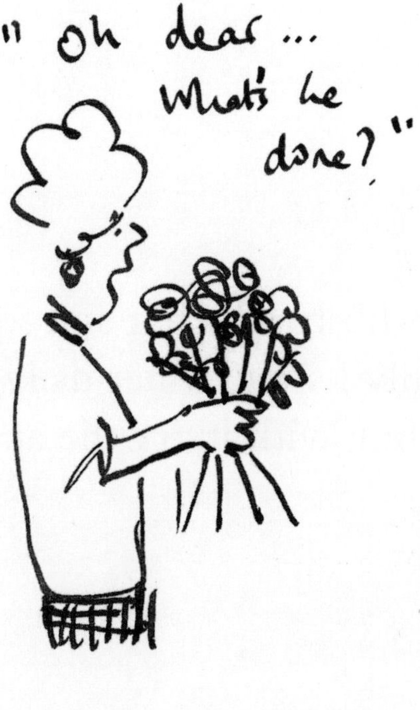
"Oh dear ...
What's he
done?"

To the husband: Hug and squeeze her daily … and if her daily won't go along with it, try the au pair!

Marriage is one plus
one equals one.

Couples who pray
together stay together.

We saw the process of achieving union as like two stones becoming one by grinding together, the hard bits of one wearing away the soft bits of the other, until at last the fit is perfect: one stone.

—Sheldon Vanauken

When you're right, be silent,
and when you're wrong,
admit it straightaway.

Be sure to tell one another
how much you love each other
at every opportunity—or rest
assured, someone else will!

Always retain the ability
to laugh at yourself.

A successful marriage depends on two things: (1) finding the right person, and (2) being the right person.

Be true to yourself and you
cannot then be false to anyone.

———

Don't be afraid to show your
weakness—vulnerability
brings you close.

Marry only for love.

"His owning a private island has not affected my decision"

One has not gained a husband, and the other has not gained a wife, but both have gained lifelong mates.

———

Marriage resembles a pair of shears, so joined that they cannot be separated; often moving in opposite directions, yet always punishing any one who comes between them.

—Sydney Smith

If two lie down together, they will keep warm.

Ecclesiastes 4:11

For a good marriage, never lose sight of what brought you together in the first place.

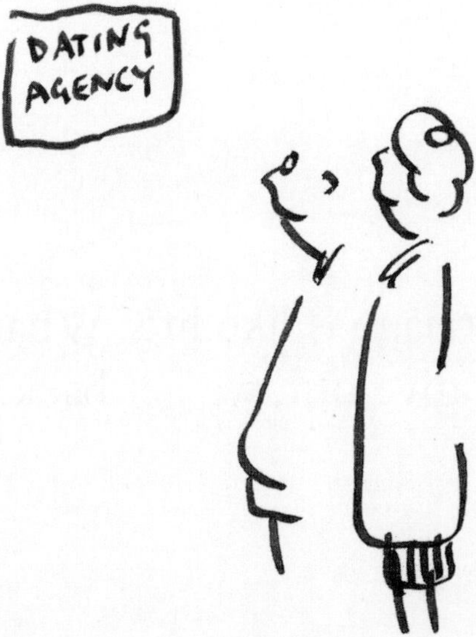
DATING AGENCY

Marriage is like life. What we give out, we get back.

Frequently listen to, appreciate,
and touch each other.

Enjoy lots of sex.

Be loyal.

————

Be considerate in all things.

————

Take lots of weekend breaks.

Don't spend the night in
the spare bedroom.

———

Never sleep on a grievance.

Young lovers seek perfection.
Old lovers learn the art of sewing
shreds together and of seeing
beauty in a multiplicity of patches.

—*How to Make an American Quilt*

An archaeologist is the best husband any woman can have; the older she gets, the more interested he is in her.

—A Witty Wife

Now you will feel no rain,
for each of you will be
shelter to the other.
Now you will feel no cold,
for each of you will be
warmth to the other.
Now there is no
loneliness for you,
for each of you will be
companion to the other.

Now you are two persons,
but there is one life before you.
Go now to your dwelling place,
to enter into the days of
your togetherness.
And may your days be good
and long upon this earth.

—Apache Wedding Blessing

A honeymoon is the brief period of time between "I do" and "You'd better!"

Rule 1: Your wife is always right.

Rule 2: Even when she is wrong, refer to rule number one!

When two souls,
which for a longer or
a shorter time
have sought each other
amidst the crowd,
at length find each other;
when they perceive that they
belong to each other;
when, in short, they comprehend
their affinity, then there is
established between them
a union, pure and ardent
as themselves, a union begun
upon earth in order that it may
be completed in heaven.

This union is *love;* real
and perfect love,
such love as very few men
can adequately conceive;
love which is a religion,
adoring the being
beloved as a divinity;
love that lives in
devotion and ardor,
and for which to make
great sacrifices
is the purest pleasure.

—Victor Hugo

Love is not merely the indulgence
of one's personal taste buds;
it is also the delight in
indulging another's.

—Laurie Lee

A healthy marriage is like a
healthy child—it looks up and
outward to experience and enjoy
all that is good and beautiful
and to love and strengthen
what is lonely and weak.

Don't wear anything in bed.

Get an answering machine.

———

Always keep a sense of humor.

———

Forget the word *never*—"You
never do this or that."

If it is possible, as far as it depends on you, live at peace with everyone.

Romans 12:18

THE MARRIAGE ALPHABET

Appreciate
Bewitch
Cherish
Delight
Energize
Forgive
Give
Happiness
Inspire
Joy
Kindness
Love
Multiply

Nurture
Obey
Patience
Question
Resuscitate
Submit
Treasure
Understand
Venerate
Woo
Xpress
Yearn
Zeal

Listen to each other.

It is the little things that make the big difference.

When you are apart, call lots to say how much you love her.

—Sir John Mills

Leave love notes whenever
you go away.

All beautiful you are, my darling;
there is no flaw in you.

Song of Solomon 4:7

RECIPE FOR A GOOD MARRIAGE

Half a cup of friendship and
a cup of thoughtfulness,
Creamed together with a pinch
of powdered tenderness,
Very lightly beaten in
a bowl of loyalty,
With a cup of faith and one
of hope and one of charity.

Be sure to add a spoonful
each of gaiety that sings,
And also the ability to
laugh at little things.
Moisten with the sudden
tears of heartfelt sympathy.
Bake in a good-natured
pan and serve repeatedly.

LAW OF LOVE

First, serve your God
with heart, mind, and strength
And then will grow love
for others at length.
Tend it and share it,
at first, with each other.
Then let it spill over
each neighbor and brother
in Christ, the family, mankind.
Thus, freedom and purpose and
blessings you'll find.

—The Reverend Ken Robinson

Love is like playing the piano.
First you must learn to play by
the rules; then you must forget
the rules and play from the heart.

There is only one happiness
in life, to love and be loved.

—George Sand

———

There is no remedy for
love but to love more.

—Henry David Thoreau

A successful man is one who makes more money than his wife can spend. A successful woman is one who can find such a man.

—Lana Turner

Be to her virtues very kind.
Be to her faults a little blind.

—**Matthew Prior**

Every day look for some small
way to improve your marriage.

Just once—watch the
sun rise together.

———

Make your anniversary the most
memorable day of the year. Do
something out of the ordinary.

———

Think of the other person
before yourself.

As you love each other, grow in the love of God. As you give yourselves to each other, God gives Himself to you. As you share your lives together, God shares His life with you. As you grow in awareness of each other, grow in awareness of God. Let His love encircle your love; let His love fill your lives. Let Him bind you as one together and one with Him.

If you would be loved,
love and be loveable.

—Benjamin Franklin

Don't marry the person you think you can live with; marry only the individual you think you can't live without.

—Dr. James Dobson

Never walk out on an argument.

———

Don't underestimate the
power of forgiveness.

———

Never forget your
wedding anniversary.

Surprise your loved one with
an unexpected present.

God is always with you; He will always love you; He will protect you, bless you, and perform miracles in your life together. Love Him together.

Treasure the love you receive above all. It will survive long after your gold and good health have vanished.

—**Og Mandino**

Put toothpaste on each
other's toothbrush.

Fetch each other a cup
of water in the night.

I'll love you, dear, I'll love you
Till China and Africa meet,
And the river jumps over the mountain
And the salmon sing in the street,
I'll love you till the ocean
Is folded and hung up to dry
And the seven stars go squawking
Like geese about the sky.

—**W. H. Auden**

The need to surrender is one
of the great paradoxes of love.
Surrender may seem like giving
up. Or giving in. But in reality
we are strengthened when we
actively choose to make ourselves
vulnerable. We are empowered
by sharing our deepest self
with another person, offering
him or her our heart, our soul,
our life. Surrender is an act
of free will. A sacred trust.

—**Ellen Sue Stern**

True love protects.

Don't allow the telephone to
interrupt important moments.

———

Do not criticize your
spouse in front of others.

Don't spread yourselves
too thin; learn to say no.

Put the toilet seat down!

Love is like a butterfly. If you hold it too tightly, you kill it. If you hold it too lightly, you lose it.

He who finds a wife finds what is good and receives favor from the LORD.

Proverbs 18:22

If the grass is greener on the
other side of the hill … it's time
to start watering your own!

Don't nag!

Tolerance and wit will make for
many happy years shared by two
people who love each other.

———

One word frees us of all
the weight and pain of
life: That word is love.

—**Sophocles**

"What is REAL?" asked the Rabbit one day....

"It's a thing that happens to you. When a child loves you for a long, long time ... REALLY loves you, then you become Real."

"Does it hurt?" asked the Rabbit.

"Sometimes," said the Skin Horse, for he was always truthful. "When you are Real, you don't mind being hurt."

"Does it happen all at once ...?"

"It doesn't happen all at once," said the Skin Horse.

"You become. It takes a long time. That's why it doesn't often happen to people who break easily, or have sharp edges, or who have to be carefully kept. Generally, by the time you are Real, most of your hair has been loved off, and your eyes drop out and you get loose in the joints and very shabby. But these things don't matter at all, because once you are Real, you can't be ugly, except to people who don't understand."

—Margery Williams

Turn off the television
at suppertime.

Dance together ... even in the kitchen in your apron!

Share baths and alternate
who sits by the taps.

[Love] is … the joy of the good, the wonder of the wise, the amazement of the gods.

—Plato

———

If music be the food of love, play on.

—William Shakespeare

———

All you need is love.

—The Beatles

The best marriage is perhaps
the one where, under the love
of God, each lays his or her
life down for the other.

True love and a hacking cough—both cannot be hid!

———

A house is made of walls and beams; a home is built with love and dreams.

—William Arthur Ward

Look round our World; behold the chain of Love
 Combining all below and all
 above.

—Alexander Pope

Help with the ironing, even
if you make a mess of it.

Keep one night a week special,
for just the two of you.

Say grace at mealtimes.

———

Compliment each other daily.

Love does not consist in
gazing at each other, but in
looking outward together
in the same direction.

—Antoine de Saint-Exupéry

There is no greater happiness
Than that of sharing life
With all its joys and cares,
As loving husband and wife.

Learn to compromise.

When asked to do the dishes in the matrimonial home, be sure to drop one or two of the most expensive plates, glasses, bowls. This should ensure that you are never asked for assistance in this area again. Note, however, if both parties are using the same tactic, this could be expensive!

Tying the knot,
As Jagger forgot,
And Henry VIII didn't know,
Keeps things aboveboard,
Lets the world know
you've scored,
A girl that you'll never let go.

Marriage is like glass. The more you work at it—the more precious it becomes.

Grow old along with me!
The best is yet to be.

—**Robert Browning**

In the opinion of the world, marriage ends all, as it does in a comedy. The truth is precisely the opposite: It begins all.

—Anne Sophie Swetchine